DOG LESSONS ABOUT GOD

By

Judy Treat

ISBN-13: 9780996291996

DEDICATION

Thanks to my husband who has always been my rock through all the trials and triumphs of the past 55 years of marriage.

A special dedication to Janice LeFebvre…a friend I have yet to meet. Thank you, Janice, for inspiring me to complete this project by expressing a heartfelt interest in reading it. I was questioning whether I should continue on or not. When I was told you couldn't wait to read it, I was inspired to finish what I had begun knowing there are fur baby moms that will understand.

CONTENTS

ACKNOWLEDGMENTS

To our friend, Devora, who lovingly assisted us with the photographs of our dogs.

To encouraging friends who convinced me to complete what I start.

To family! We all love our fur babies…

To Aunt Pat…. Flip's other mom.

Most of all: To my God. He makes all things possible. After all, God spelled backwards is dog.

PEPPER

GUARDIAN ANGEL

Our first family dog was an accident. Our children were four and eight months. Some ladies at church were moving and asked us to take Pepper. He was blonde and beautiful—a full sized, well behaved collie. He only lived with us a couple of years until we moved to California.

The outstanding memory of this dog is his herding ability for our baby Chris. Our baby boy was crawling. Little Chris would be on the steps outside, and of course, I'd be near him or watching from inside the patio door. Pepper would move his body along as the kid crawled cradling him with his big bulky fur every inch that Chris moved. I had heard of dogs herding sheep, but seeing this animal, completely by instinct, protect our baby son did something special to my mommy heart. It made the verses that God guides and protects His people meaningful and vivid.

While living in this house before Chris was born, we were asked a question that would change the trajectory of life forever. A girlfriend at church asked us to consider having a fourteen year old foster child move in with us as they had to move. She was not permitted to go with them or leave the state by law. We said yes. The girl was pregnant.

Since our baby was adopted, we got to witness an amazing process unfold. The timing was a half century ago, as I look back on it today. The biological parents of our girl were only pictures on a folder we were not privy to browse. We knew scant details, and never had names or knew much about her life.

After our foster girl left, I was amazed at the maturity of her thoughts. She watched us with the love we had for our child, and we witnessed her love her unborn baby enough to tell us she wanted to keep it, but she knew better. All she dreamed about was a family to adopt and love her babe.

I marveled when she said, "I know I can't keep my baby, but I want to hold it all the time I have, and feed it for the three days I have in the hospital. We saw in her what we hoped was a picture of the first parents of our children.

We were asked again to keep a second pregnant teen. We saw the same love for her unborn and the wrestling that seventeen year old struggled with as she drew near the time of delivery. I was amazed at the way this loving young woman was at my side every time there was a dish to be washed or laundry to fold.

I began at some point to see this young lady was not willing to give her baby up. I told the social workers to be prepared. Sure enough, when the lawyer came to the hospital to serve the papers surrendering her rights, she tore up the document. Both these young women wrote to us from time to time after they went back to their respective homes.

We realized these weeks and months with us were some of the most difficult periods of time they might ever experience.

The second girl with us begged her long distance dad to let her keep and bring her newborn home. He said no. Later, a letter from her stated all she had ever wanted was someone to love. I wondered what it would have been like for someone to nurture this wish and assist her in the effort. This teen had been formerly on a detention farm and related some stories of her difficult past. For the life of me, I failed to see obstinacy or any sense of disrespect from her in our home.

Later on, after some weeks, the agency called us to ask again if we would share our home. We said "yes" a third time to take in a woman older than me who was also expecting. Her story was particularly heartrending. She was crippled from a car wreck. She was a prostitute who had been driving 150 miles per hour. She left Las Vegas and moved back to Texas. She was also a heroin addict. Some of the young people in our Sunday school class decided to help with finding ways our third pregnant visitor could find new skills for a different occupation. The background was a bit unusual for us, and the fact that she was older by some years was different. She wanted her baby, but health and history were issues that made her circumstances impossible. After delivery, she was able to write to us about the joys of her new job. Some people had assisted in showing her how to apply for jobs and watch for openings. She was hired in a senior residence home, and loved the people and staff. Oddly enough, some of the best heart lessons of my life were with these three people. They became family for a span of time.

After she left, we adopted a baby boy three days old. Our seeing these women who ate with us and became part of our lives and helped us with chores voluntarily—made us doubly thankful our baby's moms had loved them enough to let them be ours.

It was a busy two years, and we decided to take a job for my husband out west in California. Those busy days of two toddlers and three extra pregnant people part time are a blur in my memory. The images of Pepper's protective love for our baby will always dance in my head.

I had never expected the dog. I had never considered housing some teens and a woman with such serious decisions to make. I would never have missed either the frisky loving pet or the three pregnant people that shared these moments in our home. I couldn't imagine taking a dog to our distant destination along with two tots all the way from Texas to the west coast in a car behind our moving truck. The move would mean all our relatives would be left behind. We were glad Pepper had been loved, and especially happy the people who took him on seemed to understand what a noble animal he was and were excited to adopt him. He was our first dog. Pepper taught me about a god given instinct perhaps all of us have been instilled with. He hovered. He protected our baby. He was a safeguard. He had the heart of compassion. We took him on unchosen in the beginning. He was a gift…. Our first insight as to the delights of five other dogs we would choose to spend our lives with for as long as they lived.

Some years after living in California, we went back to Texas for a new job for Dave. We said yes to invite a small seven year old girl into our family, never knowing we would say yes to the array of older girls needing homes in the near future. We began living with our youngest little person who would become part time family. She had been living with a family nearby that had taken her in. It was clear she was not fitting in too well there. It seemed she needed more affirmation. Who knows the stresses the family she was with had been coping with. They had several small children of their own.

The small adorable little tyke came to our nest. We had some issues also. She taught us many lessons in love. She had thick rimmed little glasses that magnified her eyes about three or four times. She had issues at school. She had memories of siblings. We arranged for her to go see a brother a hundred miles or so away. She and her siblings had been found prowling through trash cans looking for their meals. She shared the bedroom with our daughter.

About this time, there was a layoff at work and Dave became a home daddy. In the interim, I drug out my nurse cap and set out to work.

They hired me at a nearby hospital to be a charge nurse of a surgical ward on the evening shift. This meant Dave would be Mr. Mom for supper and, yes sir-ree...the bedtime bedlam.

One time, after I had been on the surgical floor for some months, a psychiatrist on staff there called and asked if I would become their nurse at an acute care ward for mentally ill. It was a new venture about to open below the floor I was working on. I must have been nuts to say yes, but it was different to say the least.

Sometimes changes are good, and there were lessons to be tucked away for future reference. The best takeaway for me was knowing this was not the place I'd opt to long term dwell near. People there were angry. They were abused and dejected.

God was with me the night one of the patients

came out into the visiting parlor in her nightgown. I assured her she'd be welcome if she could put on some appropriate clothing. She stormed out of there. After some hours as I made evening rounds, she jumped me from behind her bathroom door and began a throat hold. Fortunately, (Yes! Thank YOU LORD!) I was across from the nursing station and got out one loud scream before the hands tightened on my windpipe. Two strong orderlies pulled her off of me. That event and a few others kept me thankful this was definitely not my idea of becoming a permanent fixture in this atmosphere. Unless, of course, I (please God never) had to be placed in this setting as role reversal.

One evening after coming home from work around midnight, I noticed a huge chunk out of the bedroom door of the girl's room. I smiled inside and said to Dave, “rough night, eh?”) He was doing his best at supplying supper, bath time routine etc., but clearly the call to a new job for him was a welcome relief for both of us, in reality.

MACHO

LONG LOVED PAL

My husband Dave brought Macho in when our kids were about five and eight. We had made the move to the West …. way out in the Los Angeles area. Our friends laughingly said we'd be among the "fruits and nuts". It was during the hippie era. We lived in an apartment for a few months.

After finding a house and moving in, Dave came in with the seven-month old pup after work one day. SURPRISE!! Despite the name, he was the epitome of a non-aggressive canine. Anyone who wanted to rub his back was a friend. He was a beautiful Sheltie when the golden fleeced canine graced our doorstep with my husband. The kids adored him!

On some summer day after a few years … he must have been twenty or so in dog life… we decided he needed to marry the dog next door.

No, we didn't even consider them living together or having other pups—it was just a whimsy and a hasty wedding in the back yard with our kids and the kids next door with bride puppy.

As I recall, we asked a complete stranger at the front door to do the ceremony. This young man, obviously collecting for something, played along with us and complied. We had a fun time making merry and declaring the new couple matched. They went to their respective homes and we came in for lunch. The dogs never were in the same yard again, as far as I know.

"Mach" was a member of the family. He was

around constantly. He got drops of meat from little hands dangling down the dinner table. He went camping. He had a jersey on and was the mascot of the soccer team of our young soccer enthusiast. He was a gentle giant and never ill. He did have a furry coat and occasionally had a skin rash, and one tick to contend with. Throughout the dozen or so years we loved and adored him as one of us—he was walked daily and doted on by all who saw him. I think having him was such an asset to teach kindness and companionship to our children.

While living with us, we became so used to his presence that we couldn't imagine life without him. Since our families were all back in Texas, occasionally we flew back on holidays or in the summer. He probably made the car trip several times in the back seat. Macho was tenderly cared for by various people we knew which were already be used to him and adored him should we need an interim family. He accompanied us to our favorite beaches and romped in the waves. He seemed to know when to tame it down or sense our frets and would come and be near with his head by our knees when he felt we needed some doggy love.

Macho slept in our bedroom on the floor beside us. He was never one to suggest he jump on the cover and realized that, somehow, good manners earned him utmost respect. All of us adored him.

One morning we got up to take Chris to soccer when, to my surprise, I discovered the car was not in the garage. The car keys which had been on our bedside nightstand were missing. Hello!! For the first time ever, we'd been

ROBBED! It was a creepy feeling to surmise someone had prowled through the house where our kids slept and surveyed us snoozing as he made the rounds.

Macho obviously was not on watch call…although he was on the floor by our bed. The car was returned the same day however, when someone on the next block was up looking out their window in the wee hours of the morning. They noticed a strange car and observed our mustang creeping along the street stopping at various homes in a mysterious manner.

Macho missed the heist and his performance at the game that morning, but all was well. The neighbors were able to recover all the stolen goods packed in our old lime green Ford. Macho lived with us through most of our kid's lives, and was one of our gentlest and best loved of all our pets. We consider him to be heart family.

One Christmas when our daughter was home from freshman year in college, we put this tired faithful family member to rest. We left our tearful children at home and both held him after the injection until he was still. Our tears mingled with his honey colored coat. I am sure he will be romping around in glory chasing a small red ball ready to pounce on whoever in our tribe arrives first.

We learned family devotion as we embraced this seven-month old gift and nurtured him throughout the growing up years of our children. He was gentle and obedient. He camped with us. He taught me how my heart would be tethered around the loyal love of this golden furred collie shepherd. He was loyal and obedient. Memories of his love for the children and how they adored him are treasured memories of mine. I'm thankful for the day Dave brought him home unexpectedly into our house. He was a complete surprise to us, but a plan of God for enrichment and unbridled love. Unbeknownst to whoever lives in that house, Macho was buried in our back yard with full reverent military like honors.

TIGER'S TRAGEDY

Here we are again….I thought my husband and I needed a dog. We were well into middle age now and it was a bit anticlimactic for me without the hubbub of some canine. Macho was gone and so was Dawn way off in college in another state. So, one bright Christmas morning, I carried Tiger to the bedside of my hubs and presented this blackish grey wriggling pup to his bewildered sleep slugged face. It didn't take but a minute to see that there was no joy in his demeanor. As a matter of fact, he had all the indications I had just landed a tissue full of nasal content for his seasonal present...or offered to give him an enema. A friend had recently announced she had pups up for grabs… and since I thought we'd need another animal… Dave would surely be on board.

He kept his gift, but the dog, though loved by

us both I think had a new male “owner” who worked all day. Let’s face it; I was his new doggie mom. Amidst those grade school years leading into high school, life was an ongoing challenge that would kind of mesh with activities of the grown up college girl and teen aged son as life roared on full throttle. Tiger was loveable. He assimilated himself into our home, and slept at the foot of our bed.

One of my most regrettable ever incidences in my life was an evening rather late when we took a walk. This dog followed me everywhere.

Unfortunately, I never thought to leash him. He never strayed or wandered off. Although I had not taught him the “heel” command, he did it. It was late at night. In the darkness, we were walking three doors from home. Out of nowhere, a cat streaked in front of us on the sidewalk and dashed into the street. I heard the squeal of brakes and the awful sound of a sickening thud. My Tiger had chased the feline into the street.

Horrified, I was too distraught to go to my baby. I screamed and ran to call my husband through the door. (great move for a nurse, huh?) When Dave came out, little Tiger had drug himself to our driveway where I scooped him up and we headed to a night vet. It was too late. This little guy was already across the rainbow bridge. We buried him in our backyard. (probably against the law but he was near) He brought us love and laughter and was instrumental in showing me that a leash is a necessity. Never again would I place a pet in such a vulnerable position and let harm's way occur because of my negligence. Both our animals had primed me to think we couldn't ever live dog-less. I learned that I was insane to not leash my precious pet. By now, I couldn't imagine life without a dog.

Our son was going through some tough teenage years. The boys on the block were into drugs. I had spent ten years with the kids and decided to take a refresher course in my beloved nursing profession that had been placed on hold. I'd had a mom who had to work all my life and my dream was staying home as long as I wanted to. Being there with our children had been a priority, but it was time to return to a job I looked forward to and loved.

Tiger taught me I needed to be aware of the harm of ignoring safety precautions and how the unforeseen tragedy could swoop down and cause irrevocable, life changing, damage. We knew his presence would leave a void.

He would be missed because of his personality and loving nature. I learned that a leash is a necessity and protection is a prime instinct to any pet owner.

As a twelve-year old, one of my favorite Christmas presents was my own parakeet! I felt so empowered to have my own personal little creature. My grandma lived with us from the day mom moved away from her unfaithful husband. She adored my two years older brother and my four years younger new baby sister. I think that was all her heart could hold at once. So, from the beginning, I knew she and I would be adversaries.

My first memory of this relationship being different from my sibling's relationship with her was seeing her in a rocker singing to the newborn sister. She was cooing a tune about them taking a train trip. I was standing there and remember asking if I could go too. She said in an adamant voice "No, just me and the baby!" There is never justification for favoritism. Although a heart may connect more closely with one kid than another in a family, letting it show is cruel.

I know this tough lady had had a difficult life. Her husband was in a mental facility. He drank, (don't know the whole story) and in those years without Alcoholic Anonymous, Terrell, Texas -- better known then as (where crazies lived) must have worked. They had lost a son at age three. I never met her husband. She and her daughter (my mom) and another son had tried to run the family bakery until her kids were grown and had their own lives. At the time grandma came, she was a seamstress in a factory in downtown Dallas. I was four at the time and my brother, also a David, was six. The tiny baby must have been only weeks old. She gave up something she loved and was good at…. for her daughter's sake. She lived in our house until her death.

That was the first year I went off to nursing school. She wouldn't miss church, but her intolerance for me was bitter and difficult to understand. Taking care of three little hellions must have been tough. My memories of a bedtime bible story, followed by her hugging and kissing my siblings then leaving the room without a backward glance at me was painful and stung my soul. She was in her sixties when duty called.

Mom had hired a babysitter prior to her coming to live with us. Once she came home to our little army barracks apartment and the sitter asleep on the living room couch. The baby was sucking on her toes. That's when grandma stepped in.

She made the dresses my sister and I wore. She made our breakfast. If it was eggs, I unlatched the screen and deposited them among the iris below. One day after school I noticed she was furious. While gardening, she'd come upon my depository. I was in big trouble. I don't remember being a full time hellion, but I probably was not the angel she needed me to be.

I think we had a couple of dogs—but never an enclosure to keep them with us safely. We never had one long term. The year I was in the third grade, I was ecstatic over being given a dyed little chick by some store for Easter…a practice now defunct. I could hardly wait to lead a troop of my buds after we went back to school to see my new charge. I couldn't find little Peeps. Grandma told me in a dispassionate tone he was in the back yard in a shoebox. My sister had stepped on him and he was lying dead in a Shinola shoe polish box on a ledge. I had my first real heartbreak at that moment. Peeps was mine to feed and enjoy for about a week…not long enough to my young broken heart.

It was long enough for me to get a taste of caregiving and owning something valuable and alive. Something I had the power and privilege of taking care of and yes! Loving!! I must have been seven at the time. It was short lived but never to be forgotten! The brief encounter with Peeps was a foretaste of being capable of caretaking and loving my service to God's creations. Perhaps only God knows what this tiny fowl had placed the seed of my forever dream of becoming a nurse? God has a purpose for all His creations, both great and small.

About five years after the parakeet present had illuminated my life, I came home from school running to my room—a duplex with a back door on my side and some windows. The cage was open and my bird was gone. I didn't see her let him out, but wonder to this day if she had done it.

Parakeets were a love. When I married David we got a blue one and named him Trickor (since we were the Treats). This little blue feathered member of the family chanted out lots of phrases such as "Trickor Treat, Gimmie a kiss, Pajarito Azul (little blue bird), Hook 'em Horns," etc. After three years in Austin where Dave was in grad school and I was beginning my career as a registered nurse, we moved to a Dallas apartment. One day a neighbor knocked at the door triggering opening the door. At that moment, a cat raced into the room. Trickor was at the edge of the dining room table staring down when the paw swiped at him. Although we quickly got the cat out and our bird seemed unharmed, we found him dead the next morning in his cage. It was the first time I had seen my husband cry. He took our little pet and buried him in a field across the street.

As life constantly offers, change is inevitable. We bought our first house about this time and adopted a baby girl at one month of age. We called her Dawn. Three years later we got her brother from the same unwed mom's home in Lubbock. He was three days old and life seemed glorious and fulfilled. My sting of infertility was a thing of the past, yet the dream of conception was never far from a hope that "someday" we would also conceive.

PUNKIN'S ACCIDENTAL DEMISE

He was a little five pounds of fur the color of his name. During my refresher course, one of my nursing instructors made it known he was available as a newborn pup. He endeared himself from day one. Our college daughter was home for the summer. Some other canine came up in our yard. I'm guessing someone dropped him over our corner fence. Our daughter begged for the newcomer to stay. I convinced her we were one dog-gers at a time.

About this time, the girl I met in the children's shelter job was moved to the same home that three smaller children I knew had been placed in. She had been beaten and used as a slave by her mom and boyfriend. The foster home was across the street from the county shelter. A man at our church lived down the street and was taking three younger children to Sunday school. One day I picked up these little ones to take them Christmas shopping. They asked me to take them for food because the woman running their facility was only giving them rice and she "ate really good food". They gobbled down hamburgers telling me of the cruelty they endured. They also said that the woman had told the teen girl she was too old to be there and put her belongings out on the street. They said this newcomer was trying to work in the mall but having no place to go was riding the bus after the store closed and they were worried about her. Later I would learn this woman sold the teens to men in other countries.

We found the teen and took her home to live in our house. David and I acquired our next to the last foster family. We loved her immediately. She had a background that filled me with sorrow. Her mother had fled from another country and was using he daughter as a cook and housekeeper for her and her man friend. She loved being with us. We adored her.

At the shelter, she was known to be brilliant in the school on the grounds there. The shelter had informed me she had one of the highest IQ's they had encountered. She loved Punkin.

One day while I was out of town for the weekend, our newcomer decided to give Punkin a box of chocolate. When I got home I discovered one sick pup. The vet told us it was too late for survival. Our newest homebody was stricken with grief. She begged me to try to keep Punkin alive. I knew the expense would be immense and Dave happened to be out of work. She begged me to see if we could try insulin treatments and shots at home. I said all right, but we didn't have success. She had offered to learn to give the injections herself. She was so guilt ridden at her tragic mistake. I reassured her she was only trying to keep up with his love for candy and was not aware of any harmful consequence.

Good news…she was offered an opportunity to attend a local college! This happy new development was welcome and just the timing for moving forward! She graduated just before we moved back to Texas a couple of years later. We keep in touch, and she has come to Texas a time or two. We see her on jaunts to California while visiting our buds where we resided for thirty long wonderful kid and canine filled years. She is happily married now. She has done well in her career. She recently called me and I was reminded of how much I admire her spirit.

There would be a pair of sisters to come to us next. No dog this time. The mom of these girls was dying. We knew them from church. By some “magical fluke” these girls had a life changing effect that profoundly changed our lives. The mother had asked us to take her girls and also had asked a younger, childless, to take their son. Since we lived close to each other we often had meals together. As it turns out, this couple had been thinking of adoption as pregnancy wasn't happening for them. Since we had done that and they were considering it—we became pretty tight. All three of these teens were in various stages of grief. Dad wasn't in the picture. The teen's mom knew that the young man would be a great influence to her son because he was a jock and hunter. They were a beautiful example of a young couple out of college and had warm personalities and kind hearts. The couple, the teen's mom, and Dave and I all went to the same church. The couple (Lynn and John) adopted a tiny boy some months later. Somehow during all this we connected closely with the new parents who also were trying to manage a teenage boy.

Today some twenty- five years later the married couple became grown up forever kids in our hearts. Later on, their little ones would be among our first grandbabies and would be in and out of our home. They adopted their baby boy first and had two other children by birth… another boy and a girl! Eventually, our foster kids (the girls and their brother) moved on—the girl we had taken into our home lived with us until a kind man at church provided funds for her to go to college. She graduated and is now a principal in a school of our former church in California.

Her younger sister went to live with an older couple who were able to provide warmth and nurturing to this sorrowful spirit. Their brother was eventually also taken by an older loving couple as the new parents became adjusted to being mom and dad to their tiny son. Our eighteen-year old son, Chris, joined the army and immediately was sent to the Persian Gulf war. It was a nail biting few months, but thankfully he came back to us and settled in Texas where his sister Dawn was now out of college and married to her husband Kerry.

Dave and I made the decision to go back to Texas where my mom was living in a residential apartment in a church run complex. By the time she came, we had adopted our next to last four- legged baby. He was a weenie dog named Scoob- short for Scooby Doo!

SCOOBY

FAITHFUL FURBALL

After Punkin died, and before the move to Texas, Dawn's toddler Maddy –our five- year old grandchild- had assured us that we would have a new dog. She adamantly proclaimed to us he would become "Scooby". Sure enough, several weeks after the move, we got a call that a friend of Maddy's mom had taken home a stray red Dachshund from the kid's school yard.

It had an encounter with their Australian shepherd (yep go figure) and was having a litter. We were invited to a pup viewing.

Maddy and Dawn accompanied us where I honed in on a tiny little baby pup with four big freckles on its back. I envisioned calling it Freckles, but a nudge from the granddaughter quickly reminded me of his REAL name.

So, we took Scooby home and purchased a bed. The tiny carpet pee-er quickly grabbed our heart –well mine from the start and Dave—surely, but a bit more -s-l-o-w-l-y.

He had a habit of wandering over when I was in the kitchen and placing his small head atop my foot. Knowing he wanted and desired closeness made me think of the same desire I long for in my connection with the Savior. The little gesture gave me the hope that God is pleased when I draw near to Him and allow Him to listen to my praises and requests.

It was magical each time our dogs connected to our family and loved to cuddle. I want to feel close with God with similar affection and sense that God finds joy when I pour out my love or need to have an answer to some concern. When we left a room, Scooby followed. If I flopped on the bed, he hopped beside me…sometimes bringing his unwanted bone to gnaw on… until he was reminded otherwise.

This rambunctious little creature doesn't always understand human logic. Going into detail is useless. He learned by tone of voice many times something was amiss. I, at times, don't get what God might be doing in my life. Logic seems to not be happening as I perceived.

Sometimes, after a decade, my mind can see perfectly what gave me consternation and even grief. A dog learns to trust, and I am still learning to lean on God's all powerful wisdom and wait until He makes plain what seemed so murky.

Scooby loved to cavort about our legs and lick about the time in the evening he was ready to go on his walk. It only took a few of these around the block trips before the time to leave became hardwired into his brain. This exaggerated energy spurt usually indicated it was almost five o'clock. He whined with joy when the leash was grabbed and we tumbled out the door. I kept him tethered to me for good reason. While walking, Scoob wouldn't yank on the leash UNLESS he saw a cat or squirrel he would love to chase.

There are pulls toward things that are unhealthy at times on my heart; but then there is control of conscience. I try to choose wisely. When I say the word "cross" he knows to go to go to the other side of the street. If I take him to a new route or a dog park, he willingly goes along. Sometimes when I find myself in a strange new path, I have to trust that there is someone up there who knows the outcome. My heavenly father understands that eventually the reason and the value will be felt, if I keep on walking forward with peace.

I have made some difficult journeys with God in my life. Infertility was a biggie. Growing up in a divorced family all my life left me with a feeling of --maybe six boys when I married and we'd all live happily ever after. It seemed to me like God plugged up his ears when after three years of wedded bliss we began to prepare for the nursery.

Asking for "whatever you will" to God seemed to work for others, but I was reeling in misery. Had I sinned so badly I was off heavens hearing radar? My empty shame and countless baby showers left my heart soured and bewildered. There were countless trips to doctors.

Finally, one discovered the fact I would never bear a child. A prior well known physician had assured me nothing was wrong. About this time in my dilemma, my little sixteen year old unwed sister became pregnant. I was over the top with confusion.

Eventually, we adopted two little newborns three years apart and had our little girl and boy.

How could I have known through the ensuing years God would send nine other girls to our doors who needed care for various amounts of time? All along, God knew best.

Not one of these would ever be unplanned by Him, and not one of them would ever be forgotten as the gifts they were to us.

These additions were not accidents, or random replacements of what could have been. He even bonused us with heart family-- the couple keeping the brother of the two girls living with us whose mom was dying. His perfect idea of family thrills my heart now, although the ache of longing in those bewildering years is still not too far off from my memory.

As a pup in the car with us, Scooby loved to be a pillow under my neck if Dave was at the wheel. Until he was about eight pounds this was pleasant, and he had a great shot of scenery.

While walking Scoob one morning (we usually went six-eight blocks), I had the thought that I hadn't sat with Jesus that morning. Is my dog more of a priority? When I got home, I did read some in the scriptures. They spoke of love. My dog depends on our nurturing care. Just as Jesus supplies my needs, I try to supply Scoob with all he needs plus one crisp bacon in his kibble each morning. He lies quietly at my feet while I fix breakfast. I see a lesson in his patience and loyalty. He knows what is coming. I try to duplicate these qualities while in the waiting room with God.

There are times while on a walk, Scooby will strain the leash to sniff some morbid pile. I also entertain some thoughts that probably aren't productive for my soul. I'm grateful to know that my God is a guide and has grace for my discrepancies. I depend on God's Spirit to pull me off unseemly places to dwell in—those non- productive places I might linger in for an inordinate amount of time. If we see a yapping monster dog looming toward us, I'll gently guide Scooby out of harm's way…even though he emits a fierce growl. He seems to believe he could beat the odds of an animal three times his size. This suddenly made me aware, this is precisely how God moves us in directions He doesn't intend us to go toward when we can't comprehend what danger lurks ahead. Often it is for our protection and guidance just as I guide Scoob away from potential danger.

Scoob has no insight as to where the destination will be if we are in the car. He has taken trips with us on many occasions, but when he sees suitcases appear an alarm triggers in him. To comfort his anxiety, he jumps in thinking he will be taken. He wants to make sure he's invited. He willingly jumps in the car at take-off. If he's included, he settles nestled in his bed until he creeps to the front to lie in the floor passenger side. There is water in the car for him if he's headed to the dog park. Rest stops keep him comfy if we're on a little trip. Although completely unaware of destination, he's in for trusting as long as we are there. It's sort of like my life. I want to ultimately end up with Heaven on the horizon. I'm assured that after this journey there is more. My needs all my life have been supplied.

Occasionally, on a walk, I will accidently drop my dog's leash-- but scramble to grab it before my startled animal gets off. Usually, he will sit down in bewilderment until my hand has it again.

I feel the same little panic when I think I'm all alone walking here. When I sit and quietly wait until I remember who is leading my path, I am reminded that God's nearness is close by and He will reveal in time what seems unsure or difficult to contemplate.

I keep close to my reminders each morning that there is never a time when the nearness of God isn't available. I, too, sit down and feel safely kept.

People we trusted kept Scooby from time to time. He loved to go to Pat's house because she loved him. Her little dog was gone and she poured her love into him, making us feel so free and safe to know that he was being loved and probably spoiled. Another close friend, Mary, is there for our next animal, Flip.

At the grocery store, invariably I would stare at the meat counter to see if there are small round bones with marrow inside. If they are frozen at home, while thawing, he seems to smell it in the microwave warming. He hovers nervously around until the prize is cooled to lukewarm before he tongues out the fatty hole in ten minutes.

My spring flowers popping up, the watercolors and beads in my studio, remind me of the thrill of joys that bring fulfillment to my everyday life. The people in my circle bring purpose, meaning, and excitement -- daily involvements. My happiness isn't a bone but a bonus of all God has done to enrichen my wellbeing.

Now and then, because of Scooby's insatiable desire to chew, I had to check the contents of his teeth to see if unwanted objects lodge there. I wonder if Jesus investigates the borders of my mind to see if various nebulous thoughts loom that wouldn't be the best to dwell on.

Shoes don't seem to be an attraction to him, although the dog will dangle one near if he thinks someone needs to put it on and get out the door with him in tow.

On one occasion I did find the little silver frame of what used to be a much loved hair comb on the floor. Each little hair taming prong was missing. Why did he not realize it was a favorite? There were at least ten in the drawer that were plastic options. Does God become heartsick at the waste of time I make or the mistakes that bring pain as He looks on some blunder that brings Him chagrin? There is the grace and knowledge that dogs don't always think twice about the enticements that lure them on.

Neither do I calculate the harm of a short reply or damage I can do without thinking something through before acting impulsively. I regret the noisy shrieks I make trying to understand at age seventy-six the complexities of the thing called "computer".

Fortunately for the dog I love, and the grace of my Father, there is restoration. God sent me the perfect mate who soothes me and shows me he understands machines and me. He forgives my outcries and proceeds to calmly unravel whatever I did to cause havoc.

I have been handed down a manual called Bible that gives me notions of how my life can be rich and full. My behavior, though off at times, is already forgiven. Christ is not a guilt measurer. The gift of life was given when I asked Him if I could be His. He is the Father I never knew. Unlike the daddy who had too many marriages, never could be faithful to mom, never helped her raise us, and seldom visited… He is always present.

Once at age of twelve or so, he brought me a

woman's dress of three sizes too large and made of an icky slicky off color that looked like it had been freshly picked out of a discard box. (Merry Christmas from daddy). Thank God, the father of the fatherless, is always faithful with His love.

If I buy a toy for Scoob, it is fresh off the shelf at the grocery store. I stand and look to see if he could chew on it and toss it in the air and pull tug with it as we play. I look for bones he could gnaw on that aren't too big or too flaky.

Nestled at the toe in our bed at night, he felt safe and part of his " tribe." He seemed to know what I was saying to him and responded after repeated renditions of various commands and comments of either encouragement or admonitions.

After about thirteen years, we could tell that

age was taking a toll on our little canine. Our kids were grown and had children, jobs, and very busy lives. It was time to take our little love out of town and spend a space of time to cuddle and relish his presence. To try and help him trust that helping him to be out of pain and weakness was not murder. Saying goodbye is tough. Loving him gently and patting him as we sat beside him soaking up the nearness was medicine to our souls. We traveled to a tiny town and small motel. No phone calls, no interruptions, no other intent than to be with this beloved buddy.

We snuggled up in the covers. We took him on short walks and told him that we loved him and he was special.

Later that week, we held him as our vet eased out his last breath. He was calm and was not resistent. So….one more up there!

One precious sight to see while he was with us was to see him curled up on Mom's bed. It truly made her day! When she moved in with us, she thought he lived with her as his chosen care angel. He slept at night in our bed at the foot end, but his naps were with his granny.

I got a sweet jolt of joy watching her be his granny. No telling how many treats she fed him when she thought I wasn't watching.

Sometimes she walked him and was so proud that he loved her wanting to be by her side. Dogs can bring such serenity to those who tenderly embrace the nurturing and lavished attention to their physical and emotional well-being. It's truly a two way street of back and forth companionship and affection. She well deserved his love.

She raised us without a man. This was hard on my older brother. He never knew sports on the television. He never got cheered on at a game. He never went fishing. He shared life with a gaggle of four females, and somehow came out as semi-normal as all the rest of us.

My mom instilled in all of us that there was hope. She trusted when there was no money to pay bills. She worked hard and kept optimistic. To our joy and surprise, she called us one day while we were still out in California. At age seventy-four she found a soulmate! She married a darling man who adored her and vice versa. They had about four years before he passed. It was precious to watch her joy and fulfillment with this kind and gentle partner.

Scooby was well loved. Never bit anyone, but could growl like a maniac at the doorbell while licking anyone that came through the door.

Basically, his demeanor was love. He knew his boundaries. He caused me to ponder what it is to be loved and blessed surrounded by people I trusted and loved. He had to have a scoop of vanilla ice cream at night with his humans.

When it is my time to go, I can look forward to life again in the presence of those well-loved people and yes our animals that impacted our lives! No fears, tears, or yelps of pain. It will be beauty indescribable, and company unequalled. I'll be looking for him when I call his name. If he doesn't come immediately, I'll know he's on my mama's bed.

In the last of her years with us, if he popped up on her bed, she felt like that was a gift and treasure. He could languish there all afternoon! It makes me smile to think of all the lessons that twenty-pound pooch placed in the pieces of our hearts!

Scooby died and I missed him. I don't know what we were thinking at nearly seventy-five and eighty, but I was sure we needed another dog.

Now Dave, he's a bit more skeptical, but willing to put up with a strong-willed wife. So, too soon maybe for him, but not for this opinionated animal freak.

We set out one bright Saturday morning to complete our family once more. Kids had gone, mom was gone, and there was definitely a hole in the fabric of my heart for some new special canine just waiting to become another family member.

FLIP…..MY BABY

We went to three places to search. We wanted

a small breed with short hair. The tiny pups at place one had scurvy—or some plague. Place number two—all pups had heartworms. As soon as we walked in at puppy rescue number three, I spied a little cubicle with "the one!" A little ball of greyish black fur rolled up looking at me saying "I'm yours!!" I ripped his card off the door and took it to the desk proclaiming he needed to be ours. Part Chihuahua, and who knows what, he is the most manic tempered little hoodlum at times. If the little buzz bomb leaps from couch to a soft chair and back—then swoops to the floor and snatches a toy in his teeth and pops back up—I ponder in wonder about his energy source.

However, if I stretch a soft wooly blankie across my lap and lift him up and croon soft words to him, he magically stills. Two of our dear friends could do the same with him, causing me to see the affection they had for him and increasing mine as they believed in his ability to eventually settle down.

While sitting around in a bible study in our home they wanted him to be with us instead of crying pitifully in the bedroom without access to humans. So, sometimes he entered the circle cuddling up in the lap of one of our visitors (or his mom) if I thought he was too wiggly.

Similarly, if I open my bible and find a comforting passage, I discover afresh how anxiety abates. When we lived in California, walking on the beach had some magical pull on my soul. I just began to pour out songs and prayers and could sense God's calming in an overwhelming manner. Calmness to Flip is nearness to his human family. It seems to be a two-way street. Calmness to my soul is to be in the nearness of God.

After a couple months of enduring his frenetic bouts of boundless exertion, we wondered if this purchase was the wisest plan for our senior aged tolerance level. I never thought of caging him despite the raves of those who swear they get to love it. This made no sense to me.

At the age of forty back in California, I was seeking a job and interviewed for the county. After being assured I was a go, I got up to leave and thinking the county hospital would be fun, a voice called out to me “You do know this is a women’s jail, right?” Well no!! Thanks for bringing that up while we chatted!!

I knew nothing about jails or prisoners or crimes. I was about to learn a lot of people in a cell are what they are for many different reasons. They all seemed to respond to respect.

Some took a while to become trusting. Some needed to know their place wasn't always going to be there. Some were ill and various diseases complicated their surrounding circumstances.

As it was, the longest job I ever had (ten years) was in this place. Some wildly unusual requests were made by the sergeant up front…such as "Judy come up to admitting and determine if this is a man or a woman. Another day I get a call that someone's uterus is falling out. Upon exam, sure enough it seemed to be the case. So, I call a code two ambulance to take her to the county hospital. (yes, the place I previously envisioned I'd be on staff!) Code two is get there soon but no sirens and excessive emergency.

Next day I get a front desk admonition that this escapee was last seen running down a main highway with two ambulance attendants behind her and she got away!! Oh well, I was learning the ropes. It took a while.

One never to be forgotten was a morning, I was assigned to admitting and one of our regular repeat heroin addicts came angrily slamming the door and hit the chair beside me with a huff. I felt a bit uneasy, although a guard waiting outside the door was present. I made the foolish attempt to ask her, "aren't you tired of being here?" I told her God could help her reverse this pattern. In a scathing rebuke she turned on me with glittering eyes and reminded me that I had no clue about her life or circumstances. It dawned on me a truer statement had never been made. She slammed out of the room and was conducted to felony housing. This was a serious Friday downer.

On my drive home, I concluded this job was not my cup of tea. Thank God I was off the next day as it was Saturday. I have to be going back Sunday morning. As Sunday came around, I found myself quietly rolling my medicine cart through her felony row toward a door I was scheduled to enter to pass out their pills. As I tensely passed her cell, she began calling out "NURSE! I thought about what you said and I am going to chapel this morning."

After the initial shock, I managed to smile and mumble the word "Great." I'd have to reconsider my ideas of resignation. After ten years of learning to love this job—my longest ever stint in my career, I retired from the county and we prepared to go back to our roots in the same city in Texas where our daughter and son-in -law had moved.

They had a baby born with half a heart Tiny Maddy had endured four open heart surgeries while living in Reno where the altitude was not compatible with her condition.

Meanwhile, back in Texas we were now moved in and though we had a pool we tried to figure out how that fit in with a new backyard occupant. We didn't need to fret. After Scoob died we marveled that he hated water and never once went to the poolside.

Thanks to God all the worries about drowning were soon gone.

Flip, to this day, has never nosed his head in the water nor has anything to do with swimmers therein. He could not care less!!! Yea, thanks Lord!!

At one point in our routine medical mission

trips doing clinics around the globe in third world countries, we (kind of) seriously considered finding a new place for Flip. Travel plans now included a caretaker and trying to train him was proving to be challenging. Parting with him would break our hearts so the thought got rejected. His cuckoo little habits remind me of all the contrary little habits that God probably cringes at when He peeks at my offhand behaviors. Love doesn't give up. He was coming along after six months and endearing himself as we see hopeful changes. He was adapting and training us as we try the reverse.

I hope at this time in my life I still can learn control in the areas where I am deficient. The locked in habits of animal verses human logic are lessening. What I consider to being normal dog-family routine is ensuing.

Our household would never be the same without our beloved little seventeen pounder. Yes, we feed him ice cream also. Yes, I think if it's good for us, it will be nourishing for him. Yes, he sleeps on furniture. Yep….he is probably spoiled.

We walk around the block and try to be patient as he sniffs at all the disgusting odors he finds so fascinating. I wonder how God puts up with all the things that distract me absorbing my thoughts, deeds, and foolish notions He still wishes I'd eliminate from my psyche.

Flip has his favorite squeaky frog. He seems obsessed with carrying it around and mouthing it until the inner little noise button came out; I saw it and grasped it up before he ate it or choked on it. In hundreds of ways God has protected me, I see the ways love compels us to want to try and ensure well-being for this little family member.

Sixty years ago, a minister whose wife was my teacher moved away. I would save my babysitting money and ride the bus from our town sixty miles or so to visit them.

I used to stop by their house on my way home from junior high and sit and chat with his wife. My single mom often worked late. Maureen lived across the street from my high school. She was always there in the living room ready to listen. One day after they had moved to another town her husband (my former minister) knocked at the door and asked if I would drive out to visit a family with him. It was a Saturday and he was preaching at a gospel meeting at our church that evening. Mom was home and said yes; so we set off. After about thirty minutes I noticed he was parking in a field with nothing nearby. Before I could even think he hurled himself on me at began to kiss me saying "This is how a father kisses his daughter." (How low can you go?) My hand found the doorknob and out I ran. I just remember seeing nothing to go to. I ran furiously till out of breath. I walked back to the car and got in. He took me home. I don't think a word passed between us. I told my mother and said we should call our elders. She said (sixty years ago now) that they would believe him not us. I put a note in his pocket that night after his sermon. I told him I loved him and couldn't understand why he would treat me like that. I never got an answer.

I loved his wife and decided I would visit them one more time. At fifty cents per hour, I saved my babysitting money and rode the bus to their place. I woke up on a Saturday morning and his wife had run to the store. I went down to the refrigerator and when I turned around, he grabbed me again and mashed on me a repulsive kiss. I got away and ran upstairs. I left their place and came home. I never saw either one of them again.

I think of God's protection often, now that I am older, and understand this episode in my life could have been much more devastating. I am thankful that God's limitation to the damage done to my fifteen year old heart was not inclusive of more injurious bodily invasion. I'll never know why this trusted elderly "preacher creature" would crush my heart so. Kindness and love can be lost in a flash. I don't even want an animal to feel cruelty or lack of affection or betrayal as I had that day.

If Flip gets too far off the curb on a walk, I will pull him back. If he reaches into a trash can and shreds a Kleenex to pieces, I pick up the mess removing the paper before he can swallow it. If a big dog scares him while walking, I will cross the street and try to get him out of what he perceives to be harm's way. Love protects, always trusts and never gives up. Every morning he wants to climb up in my lap. I stretch the wooly plaid blanket over my legs and hoist him up. I'm done eating, but he sniffs the table in case there is a tidbit for him. We usually read a Bible story or chapter at this point then go outside to check out the flowers and pick some for the table. He's an inside dog for the most part, but stretches of squirrel chasing occur off and on.

Flip depends on us for everything. I depend on God to see me through each day and supply my needs. Flip depends on David to put up an umbrella to cover him as he walks him in the rain. Flip cannot pour kibble in his bowl, can't open the door if he needs to go outside, can't refill his water bowl, and can't even attach his own leash to his collar to go around the block. He depends on us, his family, for all his needs, wants, and adventures.

What if we had been spirited away and were being raised by a tribe of strangers who took us in after who knows what happened at birth? Then we found ourselves in a cage waiting for someone to choose us and take us in? All this dog wants is to be near one of us. He will lick on our legs if he thinks it is time to stroll. He will stare at the door if he does not care to pee at the moment we are standing there with the door open, asking him to go relieve himself. We are his company. If we lie down to catch a movie, he will peer up on the covers letting me know to lift him up there so he can chill until sleep time in his chair across the room.

If I come upstairs to e-mail, he is in a soft chair napping. If I fix a snack in the kitchen, he wants some. I look down at the slightest clink of a dish and he stares up at me wondering if it is something that will land in his bowl.

I love Flip even though early on I would I walk into a room and find the wet telltale ring of pee.

I get the spot remover and a rag and stomp paper towels over it and spray- scrubbing the carpet clean. My own dribbled outpourings of anger or frustration are cleansed by the hanging Man on Calvary. I hope some of my unhealthy spiritual habits are dwindling as I age. We are finding fewer and fewer evidences of Flip's lack of control. If we leave him inside now longer than we think he could stand, the rugs are still dry! I am learning to wait longer on God if I think He should move a bit faster in doing what I think should be happening.

Maturity comes in bits. Evidence piles up that Flip is functioning better as the training and repetitive routines become familiar. The promised gift of the Holy Spirit is willing to renew and change the barometer of my heart toward forgiveness.

As I retrain my brain to not entertain subjects that throw bitterness and regret to the forefront of my consciousness; I am reminded of Flip entering a room to hop up on a chair beside me and falling asleep on a soft cover shutting out concerns and resting. Sometimes he flips on his back all stretched out with his head perched awkwardly to the side, legs pointing up to the ceiling. (Go figure). I, too, can fall into the presence of God and beg him to come close to me and hear my pleas for more understanding and wisdom. I desire the nearness of my Lord and Master also.

Ranking up there with a flavored tall rib bone is the aforementioned squeaky frog. After he removed one little noise maker inside the original, we purchased two more. God knows how to delight our hearts and sends blessings that surprise and amaze me at times. He fills our thirsty souls, just as I try to keep two little water bowls in various parts of the house and one outdoors for the dog.

In the morning, he knows there will be one strip of crisp bacon crumbled over his dry kibble. He does a happy dance until his bowl sets down on the floor. He heard the ding of the microwave telling him all was crispy and ready for his consumption. The Word says my ears will one day hear a trumpet and see the coming Lord taking His children to Paradise.

The worries about the pool were unfounded. We never put up a fence to surround the pool. We wondered how to go out without a fence to keep him out of the water area although the back yard was encircled already. We watched him in the yard when out a first. Gradually we noticed he never went near. He never seemed to be interested at all in being in the pool if swimmers were inside it. Sometimes the things that are huge concerns just indicate that worrying is useless when God is going to solve an issue in the most amazing way ever. No wonder we fret and let anxiety build unless we remember that we never can foresee some of the ways we are blessed and how able God is to allow peace and blessing and replace fear with freedom.

Should I mention the toys that he is wild about? He has more playthings than any of our once nine month old children could have combined at that age. Because of his incessant need to chew, I regularly discard the stuffing- (gnarled and scattered) and spilled around in a four foot circumference. The two remaining frogs still have squeakers. The original three inch felt amphibian has one and a half holes in his belly. I have sewed up their feet, and soon they will be discarded as a hazard. He goes into a frenzy with a knotted soft rag and circles the yard like his tail is on fire. Old bones are a go back to draw on, and he can finally eat the hardest one imaginable. It emerges from the other end, remarkably, in a rather stiff form…one of the tenth wonders of the world, I'm assuming along with the miracle of any teeth left after a session of consumption.

As humans we have our favorite games, favorite toys and pastimes. These vary. Forms of delight that delight according to gender, or early training or lessons, or just discoveries that causes our hearts to sing. I loved words early on.

In high school I could write whatever I wanted in a humor column in our weekly newspaper. When it was passed out last period, it thrilled me to hear chuckles of surrounding students. There are tons of diary episodes all over the house. I find joy in picking up one about a trip several years ago, and digesting each moment otherwise forgotten.

Recently I connected with a foster child who had written me once after she had been removed from my home and was placed from pillar to post; ending up in the jail I worked at as a nurse. Thirty years later, she recently began on Facebook to write me. Then she recently has moved in my city. I had carefully packed away the last correspondence she sent from Hawaii years thirty-four years prior. We ran into one another while I was on business in a meeting at the county hospital. Yep—same one I thought I'd be working at. She told me she had met a man and was going to Hawaii with him. She said she would write and sure enough, she did. While rummaging through the garage not too long ago I came across her letter. On top of it was the reply I posted to her, marked "Unable to deliver".

I had felt guilt that there was so much disturbance in our home while she was there, that we made the decision we needed to have her go. She was living with agony of lifelong years of child abuse. Shortly after I saw her many long years ago, she wrote me that she was doing so much better and she added “my psychiatrist told me the only happy memories in my head were in your home.”

God never forgets and finds ways to surprise and delight. Jayna and I still need one another, perhaps now more than ever. Her way has been difficult. A car wreck has left her health compromised. She is a widow—husband killed in a drug related violent incident.

Unlike many other children who lived with us “part time” who have lost track of us or the other way around, it has been sweet to connect the dots of how our lives have diverged. We had made the difficult decision that Jayna was too disruptive on our children as well as our household peace those long years ago. She had turned in her dad for years of incest. She failed the group home after leaving our house and she's the one I saw in jail calling me "MOM".

I felt immense failure and guilt that we had not been able to cope while she lived in our home. God is all about fresh starts.

Favorites… One of my best "toys" in my grown-up life is beads. Making them into earrings and bracelets and finding a perfect chain to go with some drop gives me a buzz. I market them in consignment shops and sponsor a small girl in Haiti with proceeds. As a nurse, I have gone to her country many times to do a clinic and have had the occasion to meet her in her orphanage twice now.

One of the gifts God provides me with is a love for giving. As a child brought up in meager circumstances, I feel thankful that I can buy a flower to give to someone who needs a touch of love. Or, I can enclose a little piece of jewelry in an envelope and mail it to a sick friend. Favorite pastimes that are free and supply joy are a simple hike in the back yard. I might smile if I see a purple bloom or the gardenia or a fragrance filled plant spiking up with odor flying up to my nose before even stooping down near the stalk.

My husband and I have had the means to take trips in many parts of the world. Flip has, of yet, not gone far from our neighborhood. As a child growing up in Dallas with my single mom, the biggest adventure of my growing up years was a trip to Austin with an overnight in a motel with a POOL!

As adults, we have seen many countries—some

on our own and some with teams performing clinics in third world countries. My life has been enhanced a hundred times over by each of these tours –sometimes to affluence and amazing beauty and sometimes to abject poverty.

Each evening, Flip, Dave and I head out the door for what has now become the second walk he has each day. He doesn't want to keep pace with me if his delicate nose smells a spot in the grass he wants to linger over. I can bet it is not perfume from a nearby rose. What appears disgusting to me obviously is heartily enticing to him. I manage to tug him away by a low whistle or words of admonishment. After all who is this walk for anyhow? (Both of us really—I know).

I wonder how many times I linger over my

computer game of scrabble until God wants to scream "DO SOMETHING more constructive"! I tell myself I am sharpening my brain. Or, I may be in some depressive mode and wasting time is all I have energy to do.

Usually we continue as three companions, and I notice he eventually comes at our compelling. I hope I hear God pacing me—pulling me off paths of non-productive involvement and urging me by His Spirit to move to areas He thinks would be more worthwhile.

If Flip comes up putting his paws on my legs, I pull up the softie blanket over my lap and scoop him up. I've finished breakfast and he usually needs a cuddle. He is also wanting to sniff the table edge and I have to remind him that there is nothing up there I want him to have. I'm also prone, while pouring over my Bible, to find some sudden distraction that allows me to turn away from focusing.

It is becoming clearer and clearer that I am crazy about Flip. I find myself sneaking him a bite of human food when I am nearly finished with my sandwich…hopefully when Dave is not looking. I feel protective and maternal for this infantile pup.

I wonder how it would feel if I was adopted by a tribe of animals and had no way to learn how to speak or be with other humans. I keep wanting to add a piece of lunchmeat to his food dish because I see his reaction when I do. I would not like to have a bowl of rice every day with nothing else even though, of course, books say not to do it.

Last night a group that regularly meets in our home was in the living room and he was quiet for an hour or two, but set up a mournful howl afterwards. We all ignored it for a minute or so. The two doggie lovers in the room kept looking at me saying telepathically—GO GET HIM! So, I did.

After all, locking me up away from a meeting would not be fun even if someone did make me a peanut butter cone a (rubber little round hollow object designed to be a treat when someone stuffs some of the brown stuff inside for a dog to lick out.) He can do it in five minutes but it was something that made me feel better before the doorbell began to sound and our guests arrived and we began our session. I also gave him a flavored bone that kept him quiet for quite a while. I finally went to his rescue and, knowing one of the doggie lovers would hold him and settle him down, pointed them to his blanket in a basket near them.

Now our kids are grown and we have grandkids. But if you love your pets and you are a mommy then you understand. He is all we have small enough around here to spoil. As a kid, we only had one or two dogs I remember and because we moved often wherever our single mom could afford. We didn't have a fenced yard and never had a dog with us for a long period of time. I don't suppose sixty years ago the average family knew vets existed much less expensive vaccines.

Remember I told you about that parakeet present at age twelve? It really WAS one of the best presents ever. Our first pet after marriage was a bird and he was tamed and just like family. We had him for several years. One day after we moved to a small apartment, a little elderly lady knocked on the door. There was no screen and when I opened it a cat roared in and the bird "Trickor Treat" was on the edge of the dining table peering down at the feline. With one swipe of his razor paw, before I grabbed him and expelled him from the home-he had left his mark. I didn't see any damage but our beloved bird was dead in his little cage when we woke up the next morning. We had been married there years and that was the first day I ever had seen tears on the face of my husband. He took Trickor to a field across the street and buried him.

When I think of being in God's family, I ponder what this is like in some ways that are difficult for me to grasp. My belief is that I am a child of His. The bible speaks of me as adopted into His care and love. I get that because we were unable to bear children and we adopted two babies three years apart. Although I wondered if our parents would love these kids the same as sibling's children, it didn't take long for me to see that love was more than giving birth. As soon as we flew home to Dallas with our one-month old little girl, mom had her in the kitchen sink to give her a bath and I was left to figure out how I was going to make formula without contaminating it.

As a nurse, it's my nature to nurture. Just today, Dave and I had a movie date and he dropped me by a store that I knew had low markdowns on gifts. Christmas and some family birthdays are ahead so I found some items and one of them was a stuffed toy for guess who! Even knowing his propensity to destroy small green stuffed things it popped up on the counter just in case it could be a hit.

If we are leaving the house, we see to it to try and let Flip outside for a while. He prefers the house when we're gone. If it's not too hot and summertime or if it's daytime and pretty weather, we set his little soft bed outside or just let him understand its outdoor recreation time. Someone gave us a beautiful doghouse, but this strange little creature treats it like a diseased gas chamber and has of yet to go inside. I'm sure there are adventures I snubbed my nose at in times past opportunities from God I could have grown by grabbing. Good gifts that He offered, but due to apprehension, or looking at other options, somehow, I overlooked them.

Ironically, a few days ago, a stray cat brought her brood to rest behind the unused doghouse. Flip kept sniffing around it and inside it until I peeped behind it and saw some tiny tails swishing about. Mama cat left them while out doing who knew what.

I was already trying to get the house in order and unpack things as we had been gone for a few days. A nice young college guy had done a great job of dog sitting. I was having a dozen women over the next day for games and a cooked meal so the last thing on my plate I dreamed of handling was a nest of four unattended baby cat fur balls. We had a dinner date in an hour with a daughter and her hubby, so I frantically began to call pet rescue places that might tell me they'd magically appear in a coach driven by white horses and scoop up the orphans. Guess what—it was 6:00 pm on a Sunday evening and the places future hope were closed on Mondays God has a funny way of helping me experience settling down and watching Him perform miracles.

I began to prowl through drawers for a syringe to milk feed and wondered what on earth this had to happen when the timing was the all-time ultimate worst. BUT! Thanks to Flip's nose to alert me of a doghouse issue and my daughter's friend who rescues cats (could this really be true????!!!!) A phone call at nine thirty at night was another miracle in our book of several. During dinner our daughter remembered a former co-worker and gave me her number. Mother cat had rescued three of her litter but left a lone little stray behind the doghouse in the dark next time we looked. The cat angel offered to send her boyfriend out to get the lone kitty from a meeting place NEAR our home and around ten that evening when the tiny transfer was done. Whew! Why do I panic when Jesus is watching over me? Dawn's cat expert friend told me the mommy cat sometimes would forsake a sick baby. It happens in humans also.

Once in the jail, I consulted with the doctor

about witnessing an abortion. I was preparing a talk for teens at a summer camp about sex and alternatives that could be chosen other than surgical removal of a fetus. The approval was given me. The young inmate was twenty-one and having her third procedure. I watched in horror at the baby being surgically arranged on a table like a jigsaw puzzle. I thought of the young girls who had arranged for me to know motherhood and could not imagine my life without these gifts. I remembered the girls we had the privilege of keeping in the interim before they had the heart to let someone more capable to raise their most precious gifts ever.

Last night I couldn't sleep. There was nothing on my mind but I'd napped a bit while watching a movie. Still kept waking up. I crept into the kitchen and ate a little tart and sat down in the dark on the living room couch. After a few minutes a little brown form appeared and hopped up beside me. He always just wants to be where his people are. I loved on him and he settled down and snuggled a bit until I picked him up and deposited him in the chair by our bed he has adopted as his nighttime place….(yes, he'd prefer to spend the night up there with us but we are old now and want the bed to remain exclusively ours) I often imagine that God is happy when I talk to him on a walk and let Him know my joy that He cares, and will hear what my joys or concerns are, and is glad that our proximity can be immediate and not from distant world to realms I only know by faith. We are the only world my dog knows.

He is completely dependent on how we care for his needs. We reluctantly have put him in a pet store a couple times if there is no person to come to our home for a night or two. We prefer the college kids that seem to love being with him if our aforementioned best babysitting buds aren't available. These older teens come and go during the day and give him walks and sleep by him in our bedroom. I leave long lists of what he likes and where his various water bowls are etc. Yes, also Wi- fi, of course, and phone numbers of neighbors and kids close by.

Doesn't God show the same concern for me in countless ways? I could never name all of the ways his providence has blessed me in the seventy- five years of life and its winding way of crooks and turns. The ways at days have been difficult but over-all at every turn He has brought me through and I have no doubt that my ultimate permanent home is waiting for occupancy.

Sometimes when I am petting Flip in my lap, I

marvel at the beautiful blend of three colors on his fur. There is dark black and stark white and a rusty brown intermingled. As I study this trio of hues, I'm reminded that the threads that make up my life experiences are sometimes dark and often brilliant with joy, and sometimes somewhere in the middle. I know I can't change what has happened that was difficult or unsettling. I also know that the light spots in my life are the good memories and experiences that have proven to me that there is a God who is interested enough in me to balance the scales of good and bad and tip them toward His storehouse of blessing.

There are in between times for sure, however, when my temperament seems to be somewhere in the middle not particularly joyous and not downcast just going along with the flow of life while trying to do the next best thing. My mind is in kind of neutral mental state like the third color in the fur of Flip somewhere between the brightness of white and the depths of ebony.

Then one morning I wake up and the elation of any tiny thrill (deep blue of a brilliant weed's bloom), song of a bird, and colors of the dawn bring me into the brightest euphoria imaginable.

Probably thinking I'm a bit schizoid? Maybe. Manic depressive?? Or semi normal?? Maybe I just have ordinary cycles of the emotional range? Who can say? Maybe there are colors in the rainbow we'll never know until eternity presents itself. I'm thankful that so far, I haven't been tossed in a cell somewhere to sort out and define my state of sanity with drugs or treatments of dubious value.

When I took the jail job, our daughter was a

senior and it was either a school ring or a prom dress. The job taught me hundreds of lessons and I loved it. Someday those stories have to come out!! Maybe that is why I don't crate Flip. I've been told that dogs get to feel comfy in their crate (it's a cell—hello) ….so I said to myself and the husband who opted for enclosure, "he will be a free canine" and he does fine on a cushion in the living room on the neck of a soft chair that has taken the form of his twelve pound body. Yep, I'm the spoiler and love this little charmer. And, no, I don't always get my way!!

A new chapter for us at home began a month or so ago. While we worked in a clinic in Haiti a few months ago, we met a traveling nurse who joined our team. She mentioned she might like to try a stint in Texas so we told her we had a room upstairs. She arrived a bit before

Christmas. In the beginning I never dreamed she had a large dog named Peanut. To say I was concerned is a freaking understatement. Flip had no dog buds. His sheltered upbringing was deficit in terms of social association. Sometimes I realize we worry about so many things that sap our positivity and are totally needless. The dogs couldn't love each other more. They tussle and tug toys and wouldn't dream of injuring each other although Peanut Maxwell is three times the weight of Flip. His owner is Jellique who is amazing and assimilating herself in our home as if she'd been in our lives for years. She has been trained in disciplining canines. I am learning from an expert what motivates behavior-mainly treats of edible nature.

Flip now lies down on command! I may walk into a room with a lesson in not storming the front door if the door-bell rings or some other appropriate doggie do good trait. Even though it seems they'd be earless or worse as they wrestle, they seem to emit a high pitched yelp as back off and let go!

Peanut is used to being crated while she is at work. Since she is on a night shift, we let him out when Dave and I hit the sack for the night and she takes over in the morning when he is ready to snooze out with her after a backyard trip for a brief run and relieving his bladder.

Peanut is clearly alpha dog with his adoring tinier version of his newfound buddy. Thanks to being around the bigger version of Peanut, Flip can go to the big dog park and not freak out at the playful interaction of other larger versions of his fifteen pound self.

Sometimes, just the introduction of some

casual, but God ordained event can stretch us and allow insight into what may be a larger opportunity to be used in some divine scheme we never may have imagined could benefit us. Having Jellique here is just another way of God saying to me, " See, you thought you were done with sharing your home but I know best!"

We had said "No more live ins now that we are elderly, but God sometimes reminds us He's not done with such and such.

Amidst having our two kids grow up, somehow our bonus heart-family bonded with ours plus about nine girls who lived with us for a number of months as the years rolled by. We never planned to adopt but infertility opened the option. We never planned to foster children, but the woman walked up to me at church one Sunday and asked if we could take her fourteen year old pregnant foster girl as they were moving out of state (rules prohibited her going along.) Saying yes just made it possible to see that inclusion was a blessing for others. Each person that came one at a time was another reminder of how an open door could be difficult at times but another reminder of sharing and trying to let God's love change our hearts and make us more malleable.

Each person and each dog that crossed our path left some important contribution to our heart, health, and well-being. The dogs have reminded us of how a higher being has control of our life plan. This God loves us and likes to send the people and animals near to enrichen and bless us at a divinely appointed time. Just as we try to please Him because we love Him, we see the same in the eager ways our pups have responded to love and care. Each little or large God lesson we learned from our dogs has been a sweet reminder that all of us need care and keeping. Our dogs taught us that the love of God and His protection and oversight are something we have the ability to pass on. It may come as a foster child, may be the neighbor down the block, or a tiny pup we see and bring into our lives.

These are special gifts of God to us as a reminder of His faithfulness, His desire to be near us, to simply commune and live with us just as our special four legged blessings desired. Keep your hearts and minds open. See the blessings great and small. Smell the fragrance of the flowers; enjoy the faithfulness and loyalty of our four legged companions remembering to thank God for these lessons.

ABOUT THE AUTHOR

Judy is a mom of three grown kids and seven grands. She and her husband, Dave, have been married fifty-five years and have now seen two of these grandchildren marry. Her first book "Here's My Heart" was published two years ago.

She has worked in various capacities as a registered nurse, and now travels to various third world countries doing clinics. Haiti is her favorite place to travel with Oak Hills church in San Antonio visiting and encouraging the people there. She and Dave sponsor a child in an orphanage there.

Judy loves teaching women and children at their church and makes jewelry at home as a hobby.

She hopes dog lovers can relate to these stories and somehow parallel how the ways dogs remind her of God's provision, care, and kindness.

Writing and journaling are frequent pastimes for her. Her other loves are traveling to other parts of the world, visiting with friends and family, and their current pet, Flip.

Made in the USA
Middletown, DE
04 August 2020

13523597R00069